How a
Market
Economy
Works

How a
Market
Economy
Works

Marc Rosenblum

1-08485√

Lerner Publications Company—Minneapolis, Minnesota

ACKNOWLEDGMENTS

The illustrations are reproduced through the courtesy of: p. 8, Pako Corporation; p. 10, Harvard University, New Office; p. 13, Michael Belshaw; pp. 14, 16-17, 24, 25, 28, 34, 59, Independent Picture Service; p. 22, Kroehler Manufacturing Company; pp. 30-31, Minneapolis Fire Department; pp. 37, 49, Library of Congress; pp. 40-41, General Motors Corporation, Cadillac Motor Car Division; p. 44, New York Stock Exchange; p. 46, United States Army; p. 51, Division of Public Health, Minneapolis; p. 64, Ramsey and Muspratt Ltd.; p. 66, National Archives; pp. 68-69, Farmers and Mechanics Savings Bank of Minneapolis; p. 74, University of Chicago; pp. 78-79, International Business Machines.

photo editor: Judith Murphy

International Standard Book Number: 0-8225-0611-4
Library of Congress Catalog Card Number: 71-84414

Second Printing 1972

Contents

If ignorance paid dividends, most Americans could make a fortune out of what they don't know about economics.

LUTHER HODGES

Introduction

The world revolves around economics. A country and its people often act in ways best explained by their economy. It is vital, therefore, to understand the principles of economics.

By studying economics, each person is able to understand his own role in the economic and social system as well as that of everyone else. Each person plays some economic role, even if he isn't aware of it.

The study of economics also helps people to understand national decisions and policies chosen by elected government leaders. In the United States, candidates

for political office tell the voters their stand on various issues, including economic ones. Some of the political differences between men running for office — at all levels — are actually economic differences. Whether to favor higher or lower taxes, for example, is an economic decision. For this reason, voters— and those who will vote in a few years — should understand what economics is all about.

Finally, the study of economics brings together some subjects that are usually learned separately. History describes events that have occurred at different times in the past. Geography covers the various physical environments and settings, area by area. Civics and social studies reveal how government is supposed to work. Economics helps explain all these things.

Each nation makes basic economic choices. Every country, or society within it, must decide how to divide up its wealth. In the United States, for example, a market economy is used. Most Americans agree that this system represents their idea of how an economy should work.

In a market economy, most things are owned by people or by corporations. Some things, such as schools and hospitals, are usually run by the government. To Americans, this seems normal and not very unusual. Other countries and other societies, however, may make different economic choices.

John Kenneth Galbraith, professor of economics at Harvard University.

Economists play an important role in society by providing the information from which economic decisions are made. Business forecasts by economists are essential for intelligent planning. Each January, the President's economic advisors must submit a report to Congress (the 1968 report was 314 pages) in which they make official projections for the year ahead in order to help guide important national policy decisions.

Economists work for business firms and government agencies, and teach in universities and colleges. Not many of them are as well known as movie stars or big league baseball players, but some, like Professor John Kenneth Galbraith of Harvard University, become public figures.

Basic Decisions

Certain decisions concerning a country's economy are made either because people want things that way, or because they make no effort to change the way things are done. In some parts of the world, countries remain poor and underdeveloped. The people have a rather low standard of living because these countries have not changed their primitive ways.

How a society's economic system operates makes a difference to each person in that society. The way people in every country live is explained by the way they answer three basic economic questions.

Most important is the first question: *How* is production organized? In the United States, most products are made in factories set up especially for that purpose. Men work with machines to produce more goods than can be made by hand. The factory work is organized and planned out. This production system is efficient and allows more goods to be produced.

A similar description applies to large, modern farms, on which the farmer uses many machines to cut his work time. Modern farm production methods take advantage of both mechanized equipment and scientific developments in such areas as breeding, soil chemistry, and insect control.

Other societies vary in the way they do things. In some countries, farmers still use animals instead of tractors to cultivate the soil. Factories are small and there are not many of them. In these developing societies, most families not only lack material goods such as cars, television, and hot water, but many do not even have enough to eat.

The next basic question is: *What* will be made? This question may seem strange to Americans. In the United States, almost everything people need can be produced and sold. If *consumers* need or want something, resources are put to the task of making it. Some nations, however, do not have enough resources to produce consumer goods for everyone. A country's resources include raw materials such as iron, oil, and chemicals, as well as the equipment and labor needed to manufacture a product.

In many countries, resources have often been in short supply. Producers find materials and parts both scarce and costly. This prevents them from turning out either equipment for other manufacturers, or consumer goods for the public.

In many countries of the world, machines have not yet replaced animal labor.

Societies have always been faced with a scarcity of resources relative to needs. This lack of resources has kept people from enjoying a higher standard of living. Their wants, except for necessary items, could not be fulfilled. When this situation occurs, the choice of what will be produced in a country becomes more real and important.

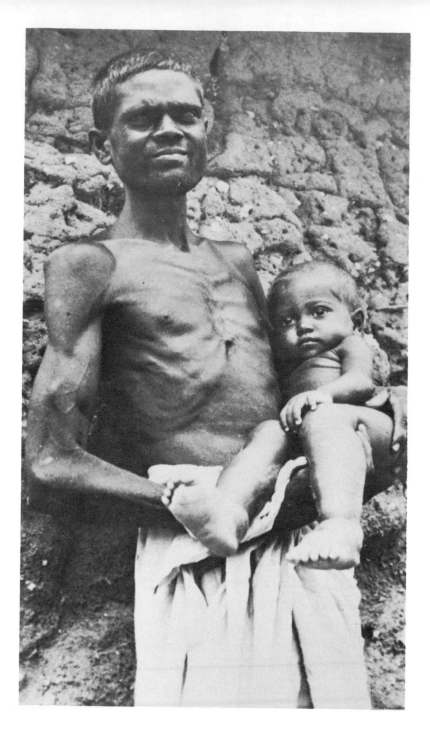

The last question for all economies is: *Who* will enjoy the output? Economists call this last question one of distribution. In America's economy, the output is distributed to people according to the amount of resources they contribute. Most people contribute their working time and effort, which economists call labor. The return these people get is called wages. Persons who have other resources — such as land — are paid for their use in different ways. These will be discussed in more detail later.

Types of Economic Systems

Related to the question of distribution is the type of economic system a society uses. The United States has always followed a capitalist system, based on private ownership of its resources. This is called a market economy, because goods are traded freely between buyers and sellers, at prices they agree upon. Decisions to produce goods and to buy and consume them are made directly by the individuals and firms involved.

In recent years, the United States Government has become more active in providing certain services for the people, such as Social Security and Medicare. The government's contributions to America's economy are mainly in areas where private enterprise does not provide services that all American citizens need. Many Americans cannot afford necessary food or health care without government aid. Since business does not like to operate in areas where it cannot make a profit, government must help those who have trouble providing for themselves.

This system of social welfare follows a pattern set by several countries in Western Europe. In England and Sweden, for example, most productive resources

are owned by private enterprise, as in the American economy, but government provides a greater number of services. This is the difference between democratic-socialist and capitalist countries.

Some people confuse democratic-socialism with communism. Under communism, government owns

Many Americans live in conditions of poverty, unable to afford necessary food and health care. Government welfare programs, such as Social Security and Medicare, provide aid to these individuals.

and runs the entire economy, as well as the political parties. Individuals must obey the state and as a result, they have much less freedom of choice than they would have in a democracy. Communism is most unlike the American capitalist system; it is a combined economic and political system and has quite different answers to the three basic economic questions.

Democratic-socialism is a middle course. The political freedom in this system is the same as Americans have, and most goods and services are privately produced. However, a democratic-socialist government emphasizes its role in protecting and caring for its citizens somewhat more than the capitalist system has done. The efforts under President Kennedy, and later under President Johnson, to fight poverty and aid minority groups point to America's gradual shift in the direction of democratic-socialism.

1

Market Economy

The Four Factors

A more detailed view of a capitalist or market economy can be gained by examining the economic system of the United States.

Resources, which economists call *factors of production*, are important to a market economy. There are four of these factors. The first, and easiest to recognize, is *land*. A person who owns land either uses it himself or allows others to put it to economic use. Land can be used for farming, or it can provide the space needed for stores, factories, or apartment houses. Payment to the landowner by those using his land is called *rent*.

The second factor is *labor*. A person sells his skills and services to an employer. As noted before, the return given for labor is called *wages*. This applies to any type of employment. (There are differences in wage rates, however, which will be discussed later.)

The third factor — *capital* — comes in several forms. The easiest to recognize is money. With it, a person can obtain the other factors from people who have them.

Capital also consists of those things which, in addition to land and labor, are needed for the productive process. Capital in this form is called *capital goods*, and includes the buildings and equipment a company uses to turn out its product. A steel mill, a distribution warehouse, a drill press, a typewriter, and a truck are all capital, since they are bought with it.

The return given to capital, that is, to those lending capital for business use, is called *interest*. If a businessman uses his own capital, part of the profit — if he is successful — represents interest. Actually, he would have had to pay interest to borrow the funds if he needed them.

The last factor cannot be identified as easily as a plot of land or a dollar bill. This factor is the managerial talent needed to run a large business firm. It is called *entrepreneurship*, a name taken from the French.

An entrepreneur is someone skilled in business. He has a special ability to bring together all the other factors, each in the right amount, to make products. This skill is necessary for a successful business. If the entrepreneur owns his business, most of his return is called profit.

How the four factors of production (land, labor, capital, entrepreneurship) fit into the idea of a market economy is best understood in terms of one individual firm. A furniture company, for example, makes chairs which must be sold at a *price* people are willing to pay. This price is usually determined beforehand. In addition, the price of the chairs has to be more than it costs to make them. Otherwise, the furniture company would lose money and not be able to stay in business.

The firm's president, or his staff, decides whether to use the company's resources or hire them in the market, depending on the cost. To build the chairs, they would have to hire carpenters, buy wood, nails, and paint, and have a building in which to make them.

It is in this context that wages are important. The amount carpenters would receive depends somewhat on how many there are available to work. If too few are in the area, more can be attracted by paying a higher rate. When there are many carpenters in an area, the company can offer lower wages and still find men ready to work.

The entrepreneurs also may choose different methods of production, depending on wage rates and other expenses. The total cost of making the chairs will vary according to the cost of each component or factor.

Demand

If consumers want more chairs, they will be willing to pay a price high enough to encourage the producer to make them. The desire of consumers to purchase a chair or some other product is called *demand*. If consumers have the money to pay for the product, the demand is recognized and considered as *effective*. Business firms only produce what they think people want to buy now, not what they are hoping to buy next year, or five years from now.

Usually consumers will increase their demand as the price of a product drops. If the price goes up, consumers generally will buy less. This may not apply to one specific buyer, who wants the item enough to pay more for it, but it applies to an average of many buyers who make up a *market*. A market is defined as all the buyers and sellers of a product who come together in a given location, during a certain time period. The market for fresh lamb chops, for example, could be described as all the housewives living in an area (buyers) and the local butcher shop (seller).

23

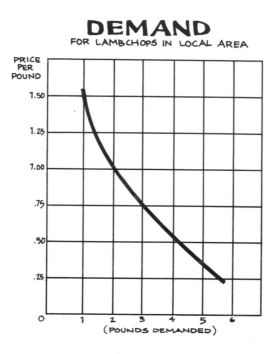

DEMAND
FOR LAMBCHOPS IN LOCAL AREA

PRICE PER POUND

1.50
1.25
1.00
.75
.50
.25
0

1 2 3 4 5 6
(POUNDS DEMANDED)

Demand Curve

The time could be several days, or until more chops are delivered.

A demand schedule could be made by asking each housewife how many lamb chops she would buy, depending on differences in price. An average of all the responses indicates that at a lower price, house-wives will buy more lamb chops. A graph of this demand schedule shows what is called a *demand curve*.

Supply

While the demand curve usually looks like the one shown on the graph, the degree to which consumers are sensitive to price changes could change the curve's shape. Items for which there are few or no substitutes may vary in price without changing demand greatly. Sellers will try to keep their price at a level where it will bring in the most money in relation to the cost of producing the product.

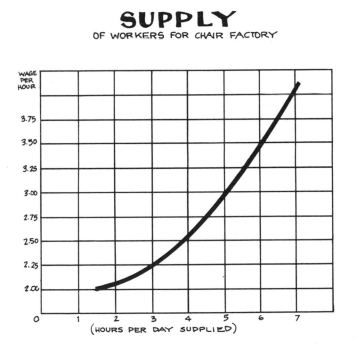

SUPPLY
OF WORKERS FOR CHAIR FACTORY

Supply Curve

The sellers' behavior can be expressed in a *supply curve*, which represents the amount made available for sale at different prices. (A typical supply curve might look like the one illustrated.) As the price increases, producers are more willing to turn out their product and sell it, even though the cost of resources may also go up. For example, if a shoe manufacturer sees the price of shoes go from $12 to $14 a pair, he would be willing to pay his workers overtime wages and increase other manufacturing costs in order to turn out more shoes.

The American economy used to be more competitive, but today many products are made by firms that sell them at a similar price. These firms compete through style changes or advertising, rather than through price.

Most current brands of breakfast cereal, toothpaste, laundry soap, and gasoline, among other products, cost the same amount. Prices on all these products include the advertising cost, which makes them much higher than they would be otherwise.

Micro and Macro-Economics

We have seen how economic forces influence supply and demand for one product — such as chairs. This type of study is called *micro-economics* (the Greek word *micro* means small). By watching just one firm selling in one market, economists hope that the behavior observed will help predict how all firms operate in similar situations.

Until just before World War II, no economists were able to explain how all the areas of a country's economic performance could be measured at once. For many years no one had even tried, because most business firms were small. It was believed that if the behavior of one firm was multiplied by all, accurate predictions could be made.

Finally, a method called *macro-economics* (the Greek word *macro* means big) was developed to explain aggregate, or overall, economic activity for a country. Some people refer to this method as the "new economics." It allows economists to measure the overall economy, rather than what any one company is doing.

Circular-Flow Model

There are three broad sub-areas, or components, within the national economy: *government*, business *firms*, and *households*. In economic terms, a household is like a family unit. It is a group of people living together, consuming (using up) goods and services. The household gets its income from whatever factors and resources its members own and make available for productive use.

The other two groups, *government* and *firms*, have been mentioned before. Government includes federal, state and local authorities.

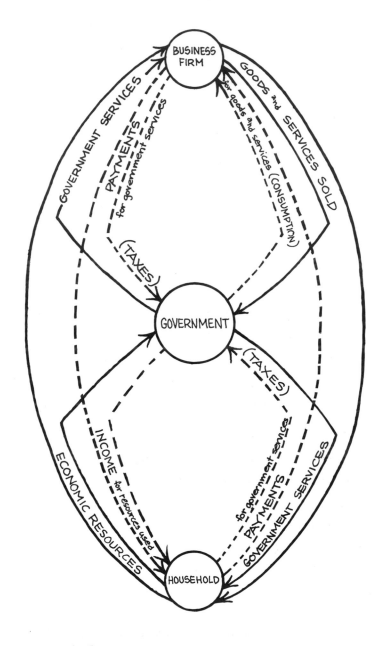

BUSINESS
FIRM

GOVERNMENT SERVICES

PAYMENTS
for government services

GOODS and SERVICES SOLD

for goods and services (CONSUMPTION)

(TAXES)

GOVERNMENT

(TAXES)

INCOME
for resources used

ECONOMIC RESOURCES

for government services

PAYMENTS

GOVERNMENT SERVICES

HOUSEHOLD

——— RESOURCES, GOODS, AND SERVICES

- - - - PAYMENTS

Circular Flow Chart

A convenient way to trace the flow of activity between these major groups is the circular-flow model shown here. Follow the arrows to and from government. Most of its money is raised by taxation. When government expenditures are greater than its revenues, government can borrow by selling *bonds* to banks, corporations, and private citizens. A bond is a promise to pay back the amount borrowed, plus interest for use of the money. The federal government can also issue more currency, or paper money, but usually does not. Other countries have done this, but the value of their money has been reduced in the process.

The United States Government obtains resources from households, mostly in the form of labor from government employees. It also buys many goods and services from business firms, especially military supplies and equipment.

In return, government pays for the goods and services it consumes by providing services for both business firms and households. Businesses make use of the government's distribution of economic data, weather reports, special tax benefits, and tariff protection, among other things.

Beyond this, government serves the economy by trying to maintain balance in the levels of business activity. This prevents severe fluctuations, which may be harmful to the nation's economic well-being.

Look at the role of households on the diagram.
They deal with both government and business firms.
Households provide resources — such as labor — in
return for money payments. They use this money to
exercise their role in consuming the goods and services
produced by commercial firms.

Fire protection is a service that households receive from the government.

Households also receive services from government. Some of the most widely distributed services are education, fire and police protection, and national defense. Not every household is entitled to all services, but there are very few not enjoying something provided by government.

The business firm deals with both government and households. Its products are sold to either or both, depending on what is produced. Money gained from these sales is used to pay the firm's expenses, including taxes. The remainder is profit to the firm. Distribution of this profit depends on the type of firm involved. (The different kinds of firms will be reviewed in more detail later.)

The circular-flow model is only an approximate version of economic activity. It does not show how fast the flow is for each line, or its dollar value. The chart also omits the process of saving and borrowing, which would add another round of lines between each group. Nevertheless, it does give a simplified picture of the main economic relationships being carried on.

2

The Firm

The differences between business firms have not been previously discussed because all firms could be considered alike, compared to other elements in the economy. There are differences between firms, however, and these are important.

Proprietorship

It is obvious that a neighborhood drug store isn't much like a car manufacturer. But differences between firms go beyond the type of products associated with each one. Most drug stores are known as *proprietorships*, which means they are owned by one man. The

proprietor may have pharmacists and other people working for him, but not many. The proprietor, or boss, decides for himself how to run his business, and he makes all the profit, if the business is successful.

Not every characteristic associated with a proprietorship is favorable, however. If the business doesn't succeed, its owner suffers the entire loss himself. In fact, if the business loses more than the original investment, the proprietor has to use personal, non-business assets (money) to make up the difference. He also has to pay income taxes at the same rate as non-business people and at a higher rate than corporations.

In addition, the need for money makes a proprietorship harder to build up. Most banks won't lend as much money to a one-man business as they will to a large corporation, because the risk of something happening to one man is greater. This prevents most proprietorships from becoming very large.

Partnership

Some of these money problems can be avoided by a *partnership*, which means that two or more people decide to own a business together. Several druggists, for example, might start a business. They would have to share the profits, but they would also split the losses, if there are any. Partners can expand more easily than a one-owner firm. Perhaps the owners could open several drug stores, and save money by buying in larger quantities.

A partnership, however, has special problems. If the business loses money and one of the partners can't pay his share, the others are *liable*. This means they have to pay, even if it is out of their own pockets. Another problem with a partnership is that each time one partner wants to leave the business, or dies, the whole agreement has to be made up again with the remaining partners. This may be inconvenient.

Corporation

Over the past hundred years, although both types of business firms — proprietorships and partnerships — have increased in number, they have become less important in the American economy. At the same time, the *corporation* has become the major type of business firm. Certain features of the corporation are better suited to a highly industrial society such as the United States.

Between the end of the Civil War and the close of the nineteenth century, the United States became an industrial nation. Manufacturing plants, steel mills, railroads, and cities were built on a large scale. This required a great deal more money than individual proprietors or even partners could raise. Another type of business organization was needed, and the corporation became widely used.

The first locomotive to cross the Allegheny Mountains in the nineteenth century. The high cost of large-scale railroad construction encouraged the growth of a corporate America.

Ownership in a corporation is divided into many small shares that are sold to thousands of different people, called stockholders. This type of ownership provides much more money for the firm than could be raised otherwise. The corporation also has other advantages. Each partial owner, or stockholder, can sell his own share without disturbing the business. The corporation can continue beyond the life of any manager or stockholder, and plan further ahead. Some of the largest corporations are busy planning what they will be doing in the year 2000, as well as next month.

Another advantage is especially important. While a large-scale business can lose vast sums if it is not successful, the most any stockholder can lose is his investment. He is not liable, and doesn't have to pay more than that. (Remember, however, that a proprietor or partner would have to share the business debts personally.)

In addition, corporations have more borrowing power. Banks are more willing to lend them large amounts, because they are more likely to pay back the loans. Corporations also borrow by selling bonds to investors. The difference between a bondholder and a stockholder is that once the bond is paid off, its holder no longer is associated with the company.

A person who holds shares of stock is a permanent part owner until he sells them. Stockholders of giant corporations do not participate in running the business in any way. The firm is run by professionally trained managers.

Bondholders are also known as creditors, or people to whom the corporation owes money. If the business fails, as sometimes happens, bondholders have to be paid before anything can go to the shareholders.

Large business corporations have further advantages over smaller firms. As the average size of individual companies continues to increase, more people are needed to do the various jobs, and some are needed to manage and direct the others. Large corporations are better able to hire college-trained specialists to plan and run their businesses. Smaller firms, unless their owners have the necessary skills, are not always run on a modern and scientific basis.

For all these reasons, the United States is a corporate society. Since so many people work for large American companies, it is important to understand how the economy works, and the place of these firms in it.

For example, about 757,000 Americans worked for General Motors in 1968. That's more than the combined populations of Vermont and Alaska! Even more people — about 3,142,000 — are stockholders in American Telephone and Telegraph Company. Actually, the majority of people in the United States either work for or own shares in large corporations.

Cadillacs running through the final assembly line. The large corporations, such as General Motors, employ almost one-fourth of all American workers.

At the end of 1968, for example, 24% of the labor force (people working or looking for jobs) were employed by the 750 largest companies. This means that almost one out of every four working people had a job with a large corporation.

Capitalization Process

Technological progress is the most important single factor in America's industrial system. New processes, new products, and improved models of old ones are the center of economic activity. All these things take money to manufacture and advertise on a large scale. While this partly explains why corporations keep increasing in size, it doesn't explain how the money is raised.

The money raised by business firms is called *capital*. The term *capitalization* is used to explain the different ways the money is obtained. Capitalization includes money borrowed by selling both bonds and shares of stock. Not all shares of stock are the same, however. The most usual kinds are *common* and *preferred stock*.

Preferred stockholders receive dividends ahead of common stockholders. *Dividends* are cash payments made by the corporation to its shareholders, usually four times a year. In most cases, dividends are paid out of profits, if there are any. Bondholders, or people who have lent the firm money by buying its bonds, are paid *interest*. This must be paid even if no profits are earned. Otherwise, the corporation may be sued in court for not keeping its promise to pay the interest. These payments are usually made twice a year.

After the holders of bonds and preferred stock have been paid, the corporation may pay dividends on the common stock. The amount depends on how successful the business has been and how much money is available.

Naturally, the company doesn't pay all its earnings out to its stockholders. Part of the earnings must go for running the business and expanding it. Otherwise, the firm would have to borrow money, or sell more bonds or shares.

The stocks and bonds of most large corporations are traded on *exchanges*. These are places where persons called *brokers* meet to buy and sell the shares. The brokers trade stocks and bonds on behalf of people all over the country. The system of stock ownership makes it easier for a corporation to sell its shares to people everywhere and, in this way, to raise sizeable amounts of capital. This system also makes it easier for individuals to buy or sell stocks or bonds quickly. People are more willing to own shares if they can find a ready market when they want to sell them.

The largest stock exchange is in New York, but there are also exchanges in Chicago, Detroit, Boston, Los Angeles, and other cities. Not all stocks are traded on exchanges. Some, usually from smaller or newer companies, are bought and sold *over-the-counter*. This market is made up of a network of dealers communicating by telephone. In exchange trading, brokers meet in person to transact their business. Either way, prices vary depending on whether more people want to buy or sell shares at that time.

3

Government

The next major sector of the economy is government, which has continued to expand very rapidly in recent years. There are many reasons for this rapid growth. Governmental responsibility — on the national, state, and local levels — is increasing. Defending the country and fighting wars overseas costs more every year. In 1967, the American military bill was more than $72 billion!

Besides defense, more money is being spent on education, health care, scientific research, highway construction, housing, and a long list of other things.

As a training exercise, army infantrymen rush from an armored personnel carrier. In past years, the federal government has greatly increased its budget allotments for defense.

The federal government has also been giving more money to cities and states so that they can improve conditions for their citizens.

America has become an urban society. Seventy years ago more people lived on farms or in rural areas. At that time about 40%, or two out of every five persons, lived in the country. Now only 25%, or one person in four, live there.

As the cities become more crowded, the cost of running them keeps increasing. The only way to pay for all the government services is with more money. Government, at all levels, gets most of its income through various kinds of taxes. But when spending causes more money to be paid out than is coming in, government has to borrow to make up the difference.

The alternative would be to raise taxes to a high enough level to avoid borrowing. Most people, however, would be against a tax raise because it would leave them less to spend on themselves and their families. Many people would like to enjoy all the services government provides without paying their share. These people forget that progress costs money.

Progress comes in many forms. Government has become more concerned in recent years with the problems of the poor, the old, the sick, and the minority groups suffering unfairly from discrimination.

Until the 1930s, many Americans believed that anyone who couldn't find work was lazy and shouldn't be helped by government. The experience of the Great Depression (1929-1939) changed that. From 1931 to 1940, the unemployment rate was never less than 14% of the total work force. In 1933, the worst year of the depression, 25% (one out of every four persons) couldn't find a job — any job.

People came to realize, the hard way, that government was needed to balance private enterprise in the economy. A healthy society requires that government help those unable to find work. Government must also train and find jobs for those whose limited education and lack of skills would otherwise leave them unemployable.

Americans today can see more clearly how unemployment levels are related to their economy's health. It is also clear why privately owned firms, each one concerned with its own fortune, cannot be expected to spend amounts in conducting their businesses that will add up to a smooth-running economy. The following is a more detailed explanation of the problem.

The Roles of Government

Government is engaged in two entirely different roles. One is to protect consumers from abuse by producers. The other is to prevent members of the business sector from using unfair economic power against customers and competitors.

Pioneers move westward across the plains. The self-reliant American pioneers established a tradition of self-interest which discouraged government intervention.

When the pioneers moved westward across our country, they were self-reliant. Few regulations limited their activity. From those early days came a tradition of *self-interest* that included business dealings. Another word for business self-interest is the French *laissez-faire* ("leave them alone"). This means that there is no government regulation of the way business corporations operate. Some people want to do business this way, even if it is unfair to others and sometimes dishonest.

Problems came up later, however, in the conflicting ideas of self-interest and *public interest*. Government acts in the public interest when it passes and enforces laws to protect consumers. For example, *laissez-faire* allows a butcher to sell uninspected meat that might cause people to get sick. The Pure Food and Drug Act (public interest) says that government inspectors can limit the butcher's right to do business if his meat is not examined. Some loan agencies act in self-interest when they make a practice of not telling the true interest rate to their clients. A recently passed law requires that this information be given to the client, or borrower.

The government, in its second role, regulates the way in which large firms use their economic power to deal with other firms and customers. The development of corporations into the strongest economic unit made this type of public interest necessary. As individual corporations grew in size, competition in many major industries declined.

Competition between business firms is healthy, because it gives consumers a choice. Where manufacturers compete for sales, each tries to attract buyers

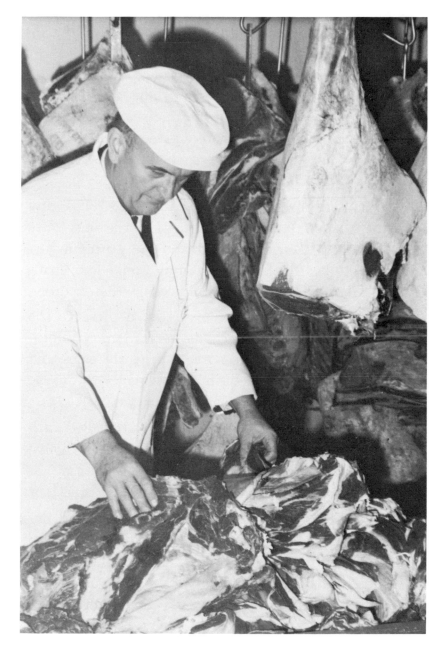

Working in the public interest, the various levels of government employ inspectors to examine all meat that is to be sold to consumers.

through lower prices or a better product. When companies become so huge that only a few of them make or distribute any item, there is less opportunity for consumers to choose between them. This situation is called *oligopoly*.

Oligopolies began to form in the late 1800s, and by 1900 a few large producers were the only ones selling tobacco, sugar, oil, lead, and many other industrial products. Today, for example, only four firms make all the automobiles produced in this country.

Congress has passed many laws to preserve the idea of competition, but the power of large corporations is widespread. Measured by yearly sales and income, most giant firms are growing even bigger.

The laws passed to prohibit a few corporations from controlling their entire industry are called *antitrust* regulations. Trusts were an old type of illegal business arrangement, but the name "antitrust" is still used to refer to all regulation of industrial practices.

In the area of antitrust activity, government has tried to protect households from business firms and to keep the big firms from eliminating smaller ones. Violaters are prosecuted by the Federal Trade Commission and the Antitrust Division of the Justice Department.

Other government agencies are responsible for regulating specific industries. The Securities and

Exchange Commission tries to make sure that trading of stocks and bonds is done in an honest and legal manner. The Interstate Commerce Commission issues licenses for trains, trucks, and buses to travel across state lines. The Civil Aeronautics Board regulates airlines carrying passengers, mail, and freight. The list is a long one. Each agency acts in the public interest to assure the safe and fair treatment of persons dealing with particular industries.

Not all industrial groups cooperate with the government. Although the United States Surgeon General has warned that smoking cigarettes is very dangerous to health, the tobacco industry is opposed to limiting its advertising. The Federal Trade Commission has recommended to Congress that new laws be passed to include warnings in all cigarette commercials on radio and television.

When business and industry are more concerned with their private interests than with the public interest, they try to avoid regulation. Many businesses employ agents called *lobbyists*, who try to secure the passage of legislation favorable to their employers' interests. The name "lobbyist" refers to the lobbies or anterooms in government buildings where legislators meet to vote on bills. Lobbyists used to talk with legislators and present their arguments in these rooms. Now, such discussions are usually carried on by telephone or away from public view.

Many times, Congressmen are influenced by lobbyists. These Congressmen vote against, and sometimes prevent, passage of stronger laws to protect consumers. They are able to do this because many people don't know or care how their Senator or Representative votes on issues that affect them.

Congress is more likely to regulate in the public interest when it has the support of consumers. Automobile safety, air and water pollution, and product quality have all been recent problems in this area. Each person is a consumer of his environment (just by breathing the air), as well as a consumer of things he specifically buys. Government's role in protecting the broad public interest against various private interests is most important to everyone.

4

Households

It should be clear that all three main groups — firms, government, and households — are closely related. Firms and government are made up of large groups of people, who also are members of households. Many people play more than one economic role.

Distribution of Income

It is in terms of households that the problem of income distribution will be discussed. All national income is divided up among the four factors of production. Table One shows how this income was distributed in 1968. This is a table of *functional distribution*. It tells us how income is distributed according to the function each factor contributes to the economy.

Table One

Distribution of National Income, 1968

Category	Factor	Amount (billions of dollars)	Percent
Wages & Salaries	Labor	$513.6	72.1
Proprietor's Income	Entrepreneurship	62.9	8.7
Interest	Capital	26.3	3.7
Rent	Land	21.0	3.0
Corporate Profit	All factors combined	89.1	12.5
		$712.8*	100.0

*Does not add to total due to rounding.
Source: Council of Economic Advisors

Look also at Table Two, which shows the *personal distribution,* or income received by each household in a certain year. There are several reasons why some individuals or households earn more than others. The most common reason is that wealth can be passed along by inheritance and either kept within a family or used to secure a greater income.

Table Two

Distribution of Family Income, 1966

Income Level	Percentage of Families
Under $3,000	14.3
$3,000 to 4,999	13.9
5,000 to 6,999	17.8
7,000 to 8,999	17.4
9,000 to 11,999	18.2
12,000 to 14,999	9.2
15,000 to 24,999	7.5
Over $25,000	1.7
	100.0

Source: United States Bureau of the Census

Another reason for differences in income distribution is that skill and ability differ from person to person. Individuals with the knowledge and talent to become doctors or airline pilots often earn a high income.

Education also counts. Those who graduate from college usually have higher incomes than those who don't. Most people without at least a high school degree are near the bottom of the income ladder. In fact, former Secretary of Labor W. Willard Wirtz has stated that machines are now capable of doing, in general, what high school graduates can do.

Opportunity makes a difference too. Many Negroes and members of other minority groups have been denied the chance to study or train for better jobs. These barriers also help explain differences in family income levels.

Table Two shows what percentage of American families earned certain levels of income in 1966. In America, an unequal income distribution is considered normal. Federal income taxes are higher as the income increases. Taxes help to equalize the income differential, but a wide range remains.

People without jobs are less able to support themselves and their families. Therefore, part of the services government provides includes ways to train the unemployed and prepare them for jobs. The Manpower Development and Training Act of 1962 focuses on retraining workers whose skills have become outdated. The Economic Opportunity Act of 1964, on the other hand, was designed primarily for training younger workers.

The problem the United States faces as a nation is to reduce the percentage of families earning less than enough to live decently. Impoverished people lack sufficient food, medical care, and proper housing. Poverty is the real cause of the riots that have hit major cities in recent years.

Some new ideas may be tried to help guarantee income to the poor. One of them is called the *negative income tax*. Under this system, families earning less than minimum living standards would receive extra money from the government. A negative income tax would actually be the opposite of paying income taxes.

The conditions of unemployment and poverty further explain why government's role in the economy is growing. Private firms can help train some workers but they do not come into contact with all the impoverished. Families in which no one is able to work must be helped by the public sector (government). In this way, the distribution of income is brought closer in line with human needs.

Since households are groups of consumers, what they do with their income is very important to producers of goods as well as to the families themselves. *Personal income* is the amount families earn or otherwise obtain. It is on personal income that families pay income taxes. The remainder after payment of taxes is called *disposable income*, which can either be spent or saved.

When the country is prosperous, and fewer people are unemployed, consumers spend more and save less. On the other hand, when more workers are concerned about being laid off, they save a larger portion of their income. Some people call this "saving for a rainy day."

When decisions to spend or to save a greater portion of income are multiplied by millions of families, the result can affect general economic activity. This total, aggregate method of looking at the economy, previously described as macro-economics, will be discussed in the following section. First, though, let's have a last look at households.

Economic Preferences

Families express their economic preferences through their demands for consumer goods and the way in which they make choices in the market. Consumer demands also provide the makers and sellers of popular items with income and keep them in business.

How, then, do consumers express preferences for community services of local government? If a community needs a new school or hospital, how is the demand made effective? This is one problem of the American system that has not been entirely solved. The economy responds to consumers who want more water skis or movie cameras, but not as easily to needs for government (public) services.

Part of the reason for this problem is that consumers buying for themselves act as individuals. Community needs must be recognized by a majority of households, in their role as taxpayers. Without tax revenues, government cannot provide adequate services for all citizens.

5

National Income

Gross National Product

Any single family or household can benefit from its economic position, when most others do not. Even during the Great Depression, a minority of wealthy Americans vacationed while many were unsure of their next meal.

This idea can be related to the overall level of economic activity. As a nation, America's concern is with how most people are doing. A good indicator is the level of *Gross National Product* (GNP).

The GNP is the value of all goods produced and sold, and all services performed in the United States during the year. The percentage difference from one year to the next is called the rate of economic growth for the country.

The GNP has gone up every year since 1954, with greater growth occurring since 1961. Since then there has been wider understanding by government officials and businessmen of some other economic relationships. Before the early sixties, there were alternating periods of high or low economic activity and rates of growth.

Theories of John Maynard Keynes

Experts had tried in vain for more than a century to find an explanation of how industrial economic systems really operated. Early economists had believed that supply and demand forces (micro-economic ideas) applying to a single firm would also apply to the whole country. They thought that an oversupply of any factor or resource would cause its price to drop. When the resource was labor, however, lower pay meant less household buying power to consume the manufacturer's products. Unemployment also cut the demand for all goods except food and other necessary items.

Finally, in 1936, the British economist John Maynard Keynes (pronounced Kānes) published a

The British economist, John Maynard Keynes.

scholarly book called *The General Theory of Employment, Interest and Money.* The long title and complicated discussion of economic problems kept most people from reading it. What he said, however, made sense to several economists in the United States. They were gradually able to explain Keynes's ideas so that they no longer seem so difficult.

In the mid-1930s, when Keynes wrote his book, many people didn't understand his theory that government participation in the economy was necessary. Popular belief still held that private enterprise could solve all of America's problems. But a whole decade of terrible depression pointed up the error in that idea. Until then, private firms generated almost all goods and services, leaving government a minor economic role. Each company, or individual firm, had no idea of what other economic units were doing. The depression showed that America's economy had finally become too big and complex to operate at random.

Keynes's system includes several important related concepts. These are discussed in the following paragraphs.

Full Employment Level

Full employment level is the amount of business activity that must be going on in order for almost anyone wanting work to find a job. The level varies according to how many people there are, and expands somewhat every year. For example, at the end of 1968, there were 82.3 million people in the labor force. Slightly less than 4% of these people were without work. The value of all products and services (GNP) was running at the rate of almost $850 billion a year. Therefore, while the economy was strong, it was short of the full employment level.

Jobless men read the want ads, 1938. The Great Depression (1929-1939) left thousands of workers unemployed. Government intervention was needed to create more jobs and thus improve business conditions.

Investment

Investment, also expressed in dollar value, is the amount business firms spend on new plants and equipment. Because these things are bought with capital (money), the investment is said to be in *capital goods*.

Savings

Saving is the portion of income not consumed by households. Money saved is available for investment if channeled into the hands of businessmen. Money placed in a savings account is lent out, or put to work, by the bank to earn interest. The saver is paid part of that extra amount.

Consumption

Consumption, on the other hand, is the opposite of saving. Economists say that anything people buy and spend money on is consumed, even though they may not use up the product.

For the economy to be healthy, it has to provide two things: jobs for almost everyone and a higher standard of living.

A rate of 2% unemployment would be a minimum because about 2% of the people are in the process of changing jobs. A higher percentage means that total business activity isn't great enough, or that some persons lack the skills employers need. Some of the unemployed have skills that are obsolete because of new ways of producing things. Some machines work more efficiently than people, especially in doing strenuous jobs.

Interior of a savings bank. Savings represent income that is not consumed by individuals.

The standard of living is measured by dividing GNP by the number of people in the country to get an average figure. This figure doesn't mean that everyone earns the same amount, or lives in a similar way, but rather it gives an estimate of how much economic progress a nation is making.

For the economy to be healthy, there must be investment spending that will give producers enough equipment, machines, and factory capacity to turn out all the goods that are needed. Businessmen spend more on capital goods when they believe economic conditions are favorable. In the general economy, there also has to be an amount of saving equal to the value of investment. This happens when households set aside the unconsumed portions of their income.

At this point, Keynes faced a big question: How can an economy composed of so many private units make the right decisions in order to come up with an equal amount of savings and capital investment? (Remember that saving is done by millions of separate households, and the total is important. At the same time, many business firms make individual decisions on investment. Nobody is told to save or consume, invest or hold back.)

If the amount that both groups generate isn't the same, the economy won't remain in balance. Should total savings exceed aggregate investment, the balance will be removed from productive uses. Total income generated, and goods produced, would be less. Some workers would be laid off. Consumption and saving would then drop. This is how recessions begin.

Keynes realized that if government agencies spent more at times of recession, their demand for goods and services would encourage private investment to rise. Government could in this way transfer more buying power to households. (Think of it as a transfusion of economic vitamins when the amount produced naturally isn't enough.) Consumption of food, clothing, cars, recreation, and everything else would go up.

What made Keynes's idea so unusual was this: No one before him had recommended this type of government spending on a large scale. Such spending meant that government might push more money out into the economy than it was collecting during a given year, thus forcing it to borrow.

Some people confused this plan with personal borrowing, and the danger of an individual going deeply into debt. Government borrowing is not the same, however, since the government represents everyone. Government borrowing is like taking money from one pocket and putting it into another.

National debt is the sum total of federal government borrowing. In years when government tax revenues exceed expenses, the excess can be used to lower the national debt. In this way, the economy remains healthy.

Thus there are three contributors to economic activity, corresponding to the circular-flow model on page 28. Households spend on consumption, industrial firms on investment, and government on what it needs both for itself and to keep the economy in balance.

6

Economic Growth

During President Kennedy's administration, the government began to accept the "new economics." The country enjoyed a level of stable economic growth never before experienced. This growth continued under President Johnson until 1966. After that, government spending increased far too rapidly, mostly to pay for the war in Viet Nam. This forced a cutback of other government programs, especially the war on poverty. Government spending also pumped more money into the economy than goods and services available, which started an *inflation*.

Milton Friedman, professor of economics at the University of Chicago, disagrees with the Keynesian theory. He believes that the money supply, rather than total demand, determines output levels. He also developed a controversial theory that a slight deflation is healthier for the economy than either inflation or stable price levels.

An inflation occurs when prices of all goods and services go up, so that any item costs more. Consumers are forced to either spend more or buy fewer things. Inflation affects everybody and is caused when the economy can produce less than people have money to buy. Consumers offer more money to try to get what is available, forcing prices up. In 1969, inflation caused prices to rise 6.1%, according to figures issued by the Department of Labor. This was the greatest yearly jump since the Korean War in 1951.

Inflation eats away economic growth. That is why it is important to distinguish between *money growth* and *real growth*. As prices go up, the value — in money terms — of output also rises. A new car that previously sold for $3,000 would now contribute $3,200 to GNP, without anything else changing.

In order to be more accurate, economists also calculate the rate at which all prices are rising. This calculation is done by the Department of Labor, which publishes the *consumer price index* every month. By deducting that portion of growth due to higher money costs, consumers can determine how much of the increase was "real." *Real*, in this definition, means *actual* output of goods or services. From 1958 to late-1968, prices of goods had increased 24%. An item that once cost $5 went up to $6.20.

Prices for services rose even more. Services include haircuts from the barber, a trip to the dentist, or any work done on or for the consumer directly. The same service which had cost $5 in 1958 cost $7 by late 1968.

Conclusion

What about the future? As the United States enters the 1970s, the country faces several important economic problems. Most important of these are the poverty and inequality that exist. Millions of Americans do not enjoy all the benefits of citizenship. Unless government, and each person, tries harder to make equal opportunity available for everyone, the economy will suffer.

As never before, steady and continuing growth is possible. The economy previously went through *business cycles,* or alternating periods of prosperity and recession. Now, by varying government spending and also government income (by raising and lowering tax rates), the economy can be made to serve the nation.

Some economic habits must be changed. Certain jobs are disappearing, replaced by automated machines and technology. Some people will be unable to find work in this new industrial environment. There will, in fact, be fewer places in the work force than people who want them. New attitudes toward these changes should be developed.

Another problem is being created as the population continues to grow. In the not-too-distant future, there won't be enough natural recreation areas left in many parts of the country. The cost of maintaining what is left and restoring sites that have been overused will add to the national expense list.

The largest cities are overcrowded. People continue to move to cities from rural areas. There is no longer a balanced population in the country. These are some of the things that young people will have to face as adults.

Nevertheless, students today have an unusual opportunity. They are growing up in an economy more able to provide for them than it did for their parents' generation. How each person participates is a matter for him to decide. Those who have studied economics will be able to use this knowledge in deciding what their role in the economy should be.

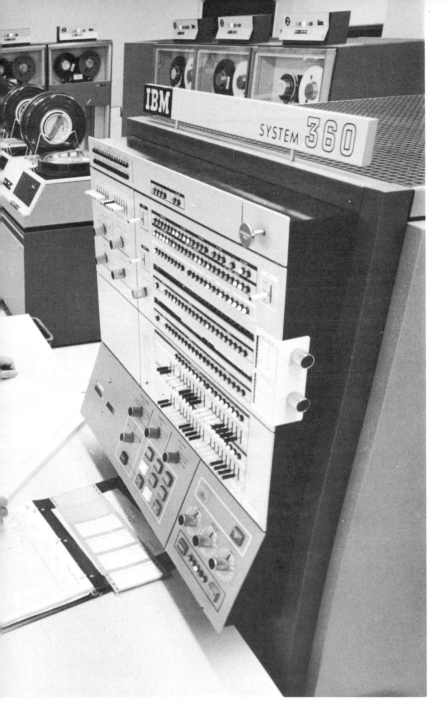

A major technological advancement has been the development of the computer. This machine makes as many as a million human calculations per second.

Glossary

antitrust laws—The regulation of industrial activity to promote competition and free choice in markets.

bond—A written promise to repay, with interest, borrowed money.

brokers—The members of exchanges who trade corporate securities, both for their own accounts and the public.

business cycles—Alternating periods of economic growth and decline, characteristic of a market economy. The United States Government partially offsets this situation by varying its spending, taxation, and total amount of money circulating in the economy.

capital—An economic resource, or factor. Money and its productive use.

capital goods—The capital used for manufacturing plants or equipment needed to increase economic capability.

capitalization—The methods used by corporations to raise capital, including different proportions of debt and shares.

common stock—The usual method of dividing corporate ownership. Dividends depend on earnings and are not paid to stockholders until bond obligations and preferred dividends are paid.

consumer price index—The government's measure of the rate of price change for consumer goods.

consumers—The users of economic goods and services.

consumption—The spending on goods and services of disposable income not saved.

corporation—A form of business organization in which ownership is transferable through shares of stock.

demand—The desire of consumers to purchase certain products.

demand curve—A graph showing how much of a product is demanded at different price levels.

disposable income—Personal income, less personal income taxes.

dividends—Cash payments made by corporations to their shareholders, usually four times a year.

entrepreneurship (ahn-treh-preh-ner-ship)—The ability to manage a business organization and combine economic factors profitably.

exchanges—The special organizations whose members trade corporate securities (stocks and bonds).

factors of production—The economic agents or resources combined in the productive process: land, labor, capital and entrepreneurship.

firm—The basic term for a business organization (includes all types).

full employment level—The amount of business activity necessary for almost everyone wanting work to be able to find a job.

functional distribution—Income divided up within a society according to the amount contributed by each productive factor.

government—Public authority at the federal, state and local levels.

Gross National Product (GNP)—The value of all goods produced and sold, and all services performed in a country during a given year.

households—Units of consumers, usually families.

inflation—The decrease in the value of money caused by insufficient goods available relative to demand.

interest—The return paid for the use of capital.

investment—Spending by business organizations on capital goods, such as new plants and equipment.

labor—The human contributions to the economic process. One of the four factors of production.

laissez-faire (leh-say-fair)—The French term applied to minimum government regulation of business activity.

land—An economic factor of production, referring to both direct land use and the space required for other business activity.

liable—Legally responsible for debts of business firms.

lobbyists—The persons employed by business organizations to influence legislators on economic issues.

macro-economics—The study of the economic patterns which affect a nation's overall level of output.

market—All buyers and sellers, and the location where products are sold, during a given time period.

micro-economics—The economic analysis of particular business firms operating in limited markets.

money growth—The percentage change in GNP, not adjusted for inflation.

negative income tax—A proposed form of income guarantee by government to all citizens. Payments would be made to families earning less than a minimum level of income.

oligopoly—A market pattern of few sellers and many buyers for certain products. The sellers are able to control prices, and consumers have little choice.

over-the-counter—A network of dealers in corporate securities conducting their business by telephone.

partnership—Two or more persons owning a business firm.

personal distribution—The income received by households, determined by the economic activity engaged in by each.

personal income—The amount received by households before personal taxes.

preferred stock—A form of corporate capitalization which pays dividends, usually fixed in amount, to preferred shareholders.

price—The monetary value of goods or services sold in the market.

proprietorship—A business firm owned by one individual.

real growth—The percentage change in GNP, adjusted for inflation.

rent—The payment to landowners for the use of their resources.

saving—The income not consumed. A source of capital for investment.

supply curve—A graph showing how much of a product is made available for sale at different price levels.

wages—The return to labor for work supplied to productive enterprise.

Index

the author . . .

Marc Rosenblum is assistant professor of economics at John Jay College, City University of New York. Before coming to John Jay he was on the research staff of the Industrial Relations Center, University of Minnesota. Rosenblum also has been an instructor at Hunter College, City University of New York, a private economic consultant and security analyst, and a freelance writer.

Mr. Rosenblum holds an M.A. degree from City University of New York and a Ph.D. from the University of Minnesota. His book reviews and essays have appeared in the *Financial Analysts Journal,* the *Congress Bi-Weekly,* and other publications.

When not engaged in academic and economic pursuits, Mr. Rosenblum enjoys skiing and photography.

The Real World Books

AMERICAN ECONOMIC HISTORY

ECONOMICS OF THE CONSUMER

THE ECONOMICS OF
  UNDERDEVELOPED COUNTRIES

HOW A MARKET ECONOMY WORKS

INTERNATIONAL TRADE

THE LABOR MOVEMENT IN
  THE UNITED STATES

THE LAW AND ECONOMICS

MODERN TRADE UNIONISM

MONEY AND BANKING

THE STOCK MARKET

TAXES

*We specialize in producing quality books for
young people. For a complete list please write*

 LERNER PUBLICATIONS COMPANY
241 First Avenue North, Minneapolis, Minnesota 55401